THE MUSIC TREE

A PLAN FOR MUSICAL GROWTH
BY FRANCES CLARK AND LOUISE GOSS

PART C

™

Lanthong Utai 1981.

© 1973 SUMMY-BIRCHARD COMPANY
All rights reserved.
Printed in U.S.A.   ISBN 0-87487-123-9

1 3 5 7 9 11 13 15 16 14 12 10 8 6 4 2

Summy-Birchard Music

Princeton, New Jersey

PREFACE

We owe an enormous debt of gratitude to our students and staff at the New School for Music Study who were the inspiration and proving ground for the new *Music Tree* series. In addition we express deep appreciation to teachers and students around the world, too numerous to list here, whose experiences with former editions and suggestions for the new series have been invaluable.

Special thanks must be expressed to our colleagues who have devoted long hours to a study of the manuscripts in various phases of their preparation, especially to Mary Gae George, Roger Grove, John O'Brien, and Elvina Truman Pearce.

Music from former editions that has proved best, both pedagogically and musically, has been retained in the new series; composers represented include Sarah Louise Dittenhaver, Jon George, Louise Goss, David Kraehenbuehl, John LaMontaine, Marion McArtor and Lynn Freeman Olson.

A special paragraph must be devoted to our appreciation, admiration and affection for Jon George. The large quantity of exceptional and delightful new music in *The Music Tree* is the result of years of happy collaboration with him. He has worked endlessly to create music that combines the strictest pedagogical demands of this plan for musical growth with the highest musical standards.

It is our hope that *The Music Tree* will provide for teachers the same high adventure in teaching we have experienced, and that students everywhere will share with our students the excitement of this new adventure in learning.

Frances Clark and Louise Goss

CONTENTS

UNIT ONE

DISCOVERY: *Major Keys*

"High Dive" is in the key of C major.

High Dive

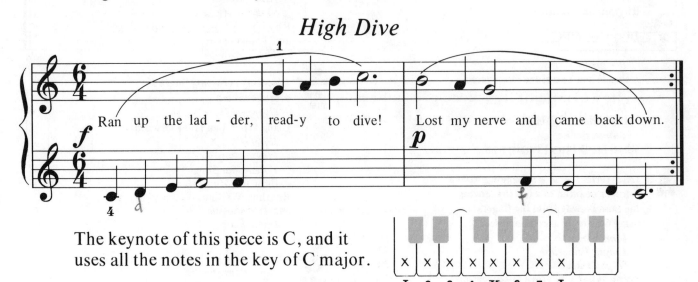

Ran up the lad-der, ready to dive! Lost my nerve and came back down.

The keynote of this piece is C, and it uses all the notes in the key of C major.

In the notes of a major key, there are always two half steps.
They always come between degrees 3-4 and between degrees 7-8(I).

Here is "High Dive," transposed to the key of G major.

High Dive

Ran up the lad-der, ready to dive! Lost my nerve and came back down.

Now the keynote is G, and the piece uses all the notes in the key of G major.

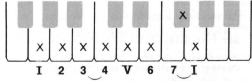

Notice the two half steps.
In G major, F is sharped to make the half step between degrees 7-8(I).

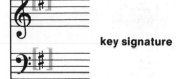

key signature

A key signature shows the sharps or flats used in a key.

Because G Major uses F♯, an F♯ is written at the beginning of each line.

"Sledding" is in the key of F major.

The keynote of this piece is F, and the piece uses all the notes in the key of F major.

Notice the two half steps.

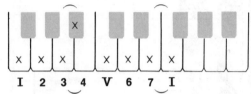

In F major, B is flatted to make the half step between degrees 3-4.

So the key signature for F major is B♭.

Here is "Sledding," transposed to the key of D major.

Sledding

Now the keynote is D, and the piece uses all the notes in the key of D major.

Notice the two half steps.

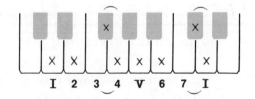

In D major, F and C are sharped to make the half steps between degrees 3-4 and 7-8(I).

So the key signature for D major is F♯ and C♯.

5

USING WHAT YOU HAVE DISCOVERED

Daydreams

[*D.C.*] **da capo** *D.C.* is the abbreviation for *da capo*,
the Italian word for "the beginning."

[*Fine*] **end** *Fine* is the Italian word for "the end."

D.C. al Fine means to go back to the
beginning and play to *Fine*.

Tall Pines

gradually louder   gradually softer

Sea Chanty

Warm-ups for daily practice. See page 62, Unit 1.

Rhythm   In each of the following rhythms, set a strong rhythmic pulse:
Tap and count hands separately (if needed).
Tap and count hands together.

Writing   On the keyboards below:
Number the degrees (I, 2, 3, 4, V, 6, 7, I).
Mark the half steps.
Check the keys from keynote to keynote.
Then write the notes on the staff.

D MAJOR

What sharps belong in the key signature? F# C#

G MAJOR

What sharp belongs in the key signature? ____

F MAJOR

What flat belongs in the key signature? ____

9

UNIT TWO

DISCOVERY: *6ths*

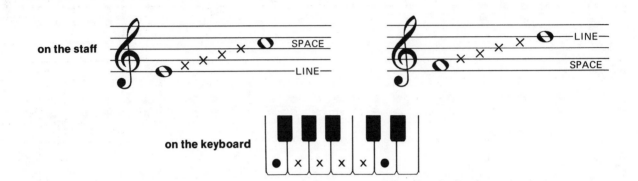

on the staff

on the keyboard

Cartwheels

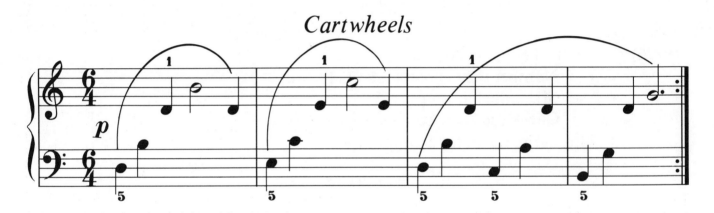

Boogie in Sixths

USING WHAT YOU HAVE DISCOVERED

Western Sunset

Bells

Old Brass Wagon

Boldly

American Dance Tune

Lumberjack

13

Warm-ups for daily practice. See page 62, Unit 2.

Rhythm

In each of the following rhythms, set a strong rhythmic pulse:
    Tap and count hands separately.
    Tap and count hands together.

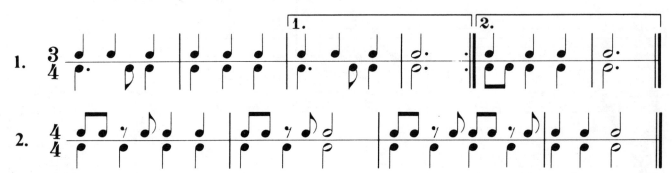

Writing

Mark all the 6ths.

Write the name of the key a 6th *above* and *below* each checked key.
    (Your answers should spell a word.)

Mark all the 6ths.

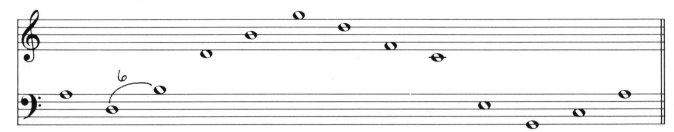

Mark all the 3rds, 4ths, 5ths and 6ths.

Write intervals *up* from the starting note.
Then write the name of the last note in each measure.*

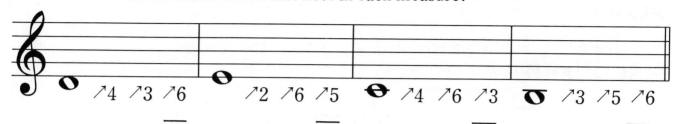

Write intervals *down* from the starting note.
Then write the name of the last note in each measure.*

On each staff:
    Study the key signature.
    Circle the notes you will sharp or flat.
    Then play the notes of the key.

On each keyboard:
    Check the keys you played.
    Number the degrees.
    Mark the half steps.

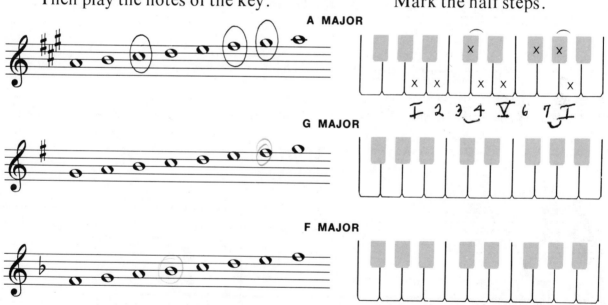

Transposing   Turn back to page 4 and transpose "High Dive"
             first to F major, then to D major.

*Your answers should spell a word.

UNIT THREE ❦

DISCOVERIES

1. Triplets

An eighth-note triplet
fills the time of
one quarter note.

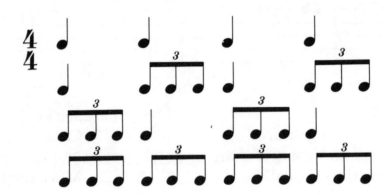

Before playing "Marching":
    Point and count.
    Tap and count.

Marching

2. Changing from a 5-Finger Position to a 6th
(by moving the thumb away from the fingers)

"Jungle Telegraph" is made entirely of 5ths and 6ths.

Circle all the 6ths.

Notice that the 6th is always formed by moving your thumb away from your other fingers.

Jungle Telegraph

3. Using 6ths in an Accompaniment

You can use blocked 5ths and 6ths to accompany a melody.

To accompany parts made mainly of triad tones, use the 5th.

To accompany parts made mainly of non-triad tones, use the 6th.

Circle all the 6ths in "Gypsy Dance."

Do they accompany parts made mainly of non-triad tones?

Is the 6th always formed by moving your thumb away from your other fingers?

Gypsy Dance

USING WHAT YOU HAVE DISCOVERED

On Parade

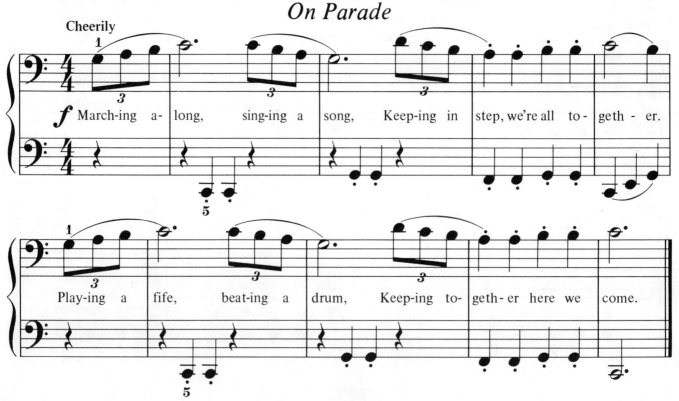

Calliope

In a Russian Village

Holidays

Warm-ups for daily practice. See page 62, Unit 3.

Rhythm   In each of the following rhythms, set a strong rhythmic pulse:
Point and count.
Tap and count.

Writing   Write intervals *up* or *down* from the starting note as indicated.
Then write the name of the last note in each measure.
(Your answers should spell a word.)

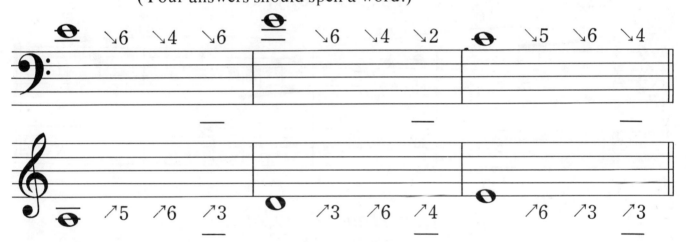

Accompanying   Accompany this melody with 5ths and 6ths.
Use 5ths for parts made mainly of triad tones.
Use 6ths for parts made mainly of non-triad tones.

Tumbleweed

Transposing   Turn back to page 5 and transpose "Sledding"
first to G major, then to C major.

UNIT FOUR 🎵

DISCOVERIES

1. Changing from a 5-Finger Position to a 6th
(by moving the fingers away from the thumb)

These two "Copycats" are made entirely of 5-finger positions changing to 6ths.

Circle all the 6ths in both pieces.

Notice that the 6th is always formed by moving your other fingers away from your thumb.

Right-Hand Copycat

Left-Hand Copycat

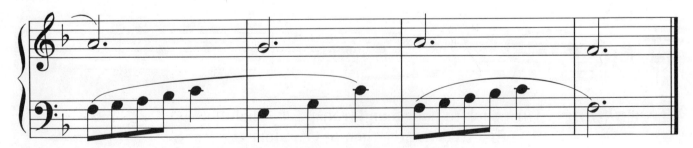

2. *More about Using 6ths in an Accompaniment*

Circle all the 6ths in "Go Tell Aunt Rhody."

Do they accompany parts made mainly of *non*-triad tones?

Is the 6th always formed by moving your other fingers away from your thumb?

Go Tell Aunt Rhody

American

Go tell Aunt Rho-dy, Go tell Aunt Rho-dy, Go tell Aunt Rho-dy her old gray goose is dead

USING WHAT YOU HAVE DISCOVERED

Cuckoo Waltz

Indiana Reel

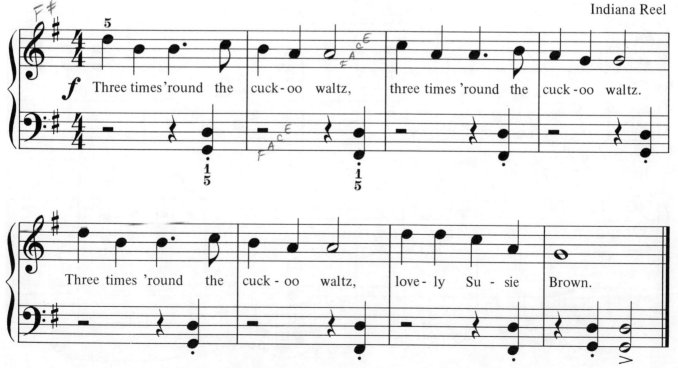

Three times 'round the cuck-oo waltz, three times 'round the cuck-oo waltz.

Three times 'round the cuck-oo waltz, love-ly Su-sie Brown.

23

Hero's Song

Notice that in this accompaniment, the 5ths move to 6ths in *both* ways.

Rumpelstiltskin

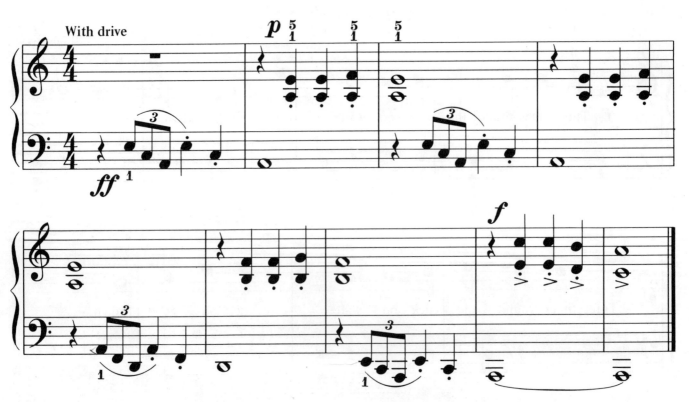

Sighing Song

Clap, Clap, Clap!

Swedish

Warm-ups for daily practice. See page 63, Unit 4.

Rhythm In each of the following rhythms, decide which hand has the harder part—then set a strong rhythmic pulse:
Point and count the harder part.
Tap and count hands together.

Writing Write intervals *up* or *down* from the starting note as indicated.
Then write the name of the last note in each measure.
(Your answers should spell a word.)

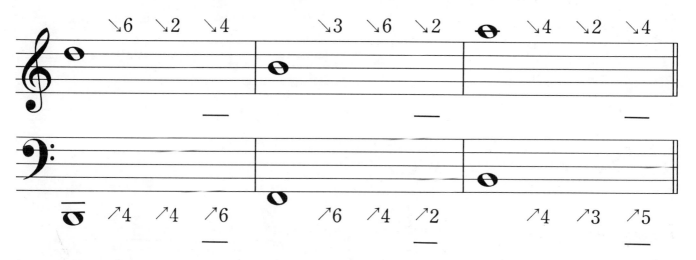

Accompanying and Transposing Accompany this melody with 5ths and 6ths.
Let your ear be your guide!
Then transpose to A major.

Go 'Way from My Window

American

UNIT FIVE

DISCOVERIES

1. 7ths

Broken Clock

For R.H. alone

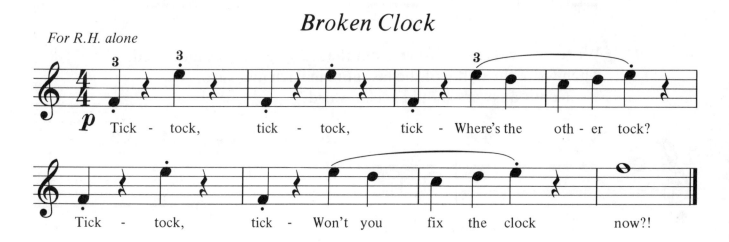

Tick - tock,   tick - tock,   tick - Where's the   oth - er tock?

Tick - tock,   tick - Won't you   fix   the   clock   now?!

2. Octaves

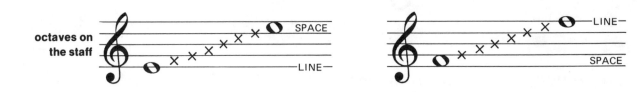

Goin' Places

For L.H. alone

USING WHAT YOU HAVE DISCOVERED

Mexican Jumping Beans

Giant Steps

Penrod and Sam

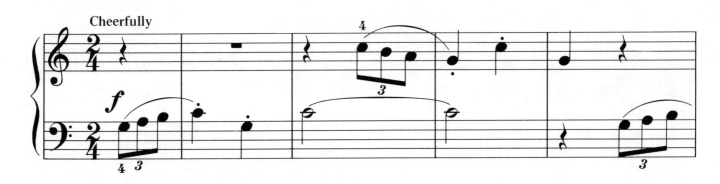

Lazy Fishin'

Southern Folk Song

Got me a hook and got me a line, hon-ey; Got me a hook and

got me a line, babe; Got me a hook and got me a line,

Gon-na catch craw-dad sure this time, hon-ey.

Warm-ups for daily practice. See page 63, Unit 5.

Rhythm

In each of the following rhythms, set a strong rhythmic pulse:
    Tap and count hands separately (if needed).
    Tap and count hands together.

Matching

Draw a line to connect each sign with its name.

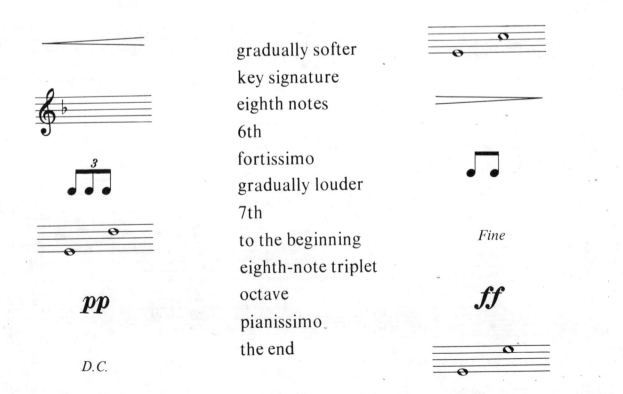

gradually softer
key signature
eighth notes
6th
fortissimo
gradually louder
7th
to the beginning
eighth-note triplet
octave
pianissimo
the end

Writing

Write the name of the key a 7th *above* and *below* each checked key.*

Mark all the 7ths and octaves.

Write the 7th or octave above each note as indicated.
On the line under each measure, name the note you wrote.*

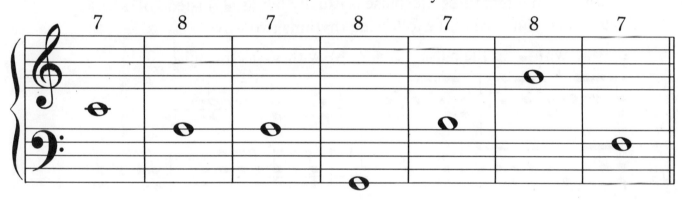

Accompanying and Transposing

Accompany this melody with 5ths and 6ths.
Then transpose to F major.

Playing Jacks

Your answers should spell a word.

UNIT SIX

DISCOVERY : *Time Signatures* $\frac{3}{8}$ $\frac{6}{8}$ $\frac{9}{8}$ $\frac{12}{8}$

In each of these time signatures, the *top* number shows
how many eighth notes there are in each measure.

In these time signatures, the pulse is usually felt as ♩. instead of ♪
Tap and count each of the following rhythms two ways:

a) with ♪ as the pulse   b) with ♩. as the pulse

The Old Mill Wheel

[𝄼·]   𝄼· is the sign for silence as long as ♩.

34

USING WHAT YOU HAVE DISCOVERED

Jack Frost

The Sound of a Blooming Flower

Homecoming

Skip to My Lou

American

Warm-ups for daily practice. See page 63, Unit 6.

Rhythm

In each of the following rhythms, set a strong rhythmic pulse:
Point and count.
Tap and count.

Writing

Mark *all* the intervals.

triad tones
non-triad tones

Accompanying and Transposing

Accompany this melody with 5ths and 6ths.
Then transpose to C major.

The Nightingale

German

Gently

mp

38

UNIT SEVEN

DISCOVERY: *Crossing Finger 2 over the Thumb*

Over and Over Again

USING WHAT YOU HAVE DISCOVERED

Jericho

Spiritual

Josh-ua fit the bat-tle of __ Jer - i - cho, Jer - i - cho, Jer - i - cho!

Josh-ua fit the bat-tle of __ Jer - i - cho, and the walls came tumb-ling down!

Playful Porpoise

Lively

Volga Boat Song

Russian

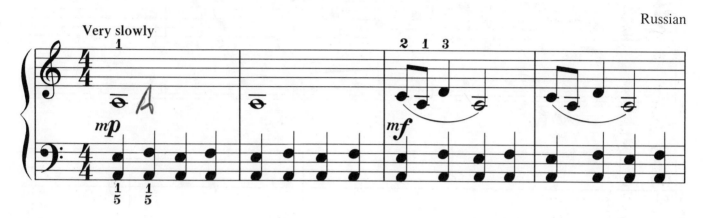

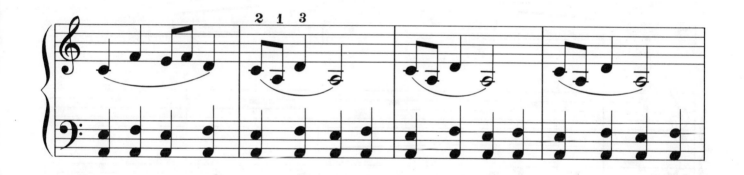

8va

41

Blow the Man Down

American

Rowdily *(8va higher with duet)*

Warm-ups for daily practice. See page 64, Unit 7.

Rhythm

In each of the following rhythms, set a strong rhythmic pulse:
Tap and count hands together.

Writing

Write intervals *up* from the starting note.
Then write the name of the last note in each measure.
(Your answers should spell a word.)

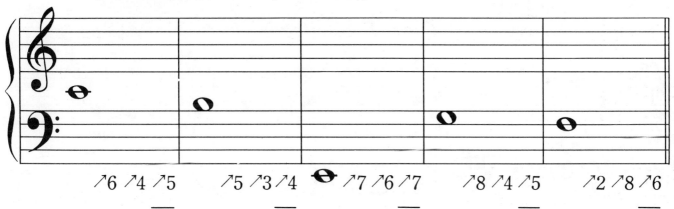

Accompanying and Transposing

Accompany this melody with 5ths and 6ths.
Then transpose to G major.

Jingle Bells

Traditional

43

UNIT EIGHT

DISCOVERY: ♩ ♪ *in* **6/8**

In **6/8** a quarter note fills the time of two eighth notes tied.

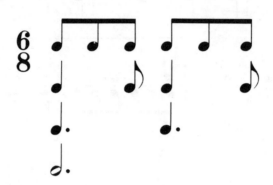

Before playing "Oats, Peas, Beans":
    Point and count.
    Tap and count.

Oats, Peas, Beans

Traditional

mf Oats, peas, beans and bar - ley grow.

p sempre staccato

Oats, peas, beans and bar - ley grow. You nor I nor

no one knows how oats, peas, beans and bar - ley grow.

USING WHAT YOU HAVE DISCOVERED

Irish Tune

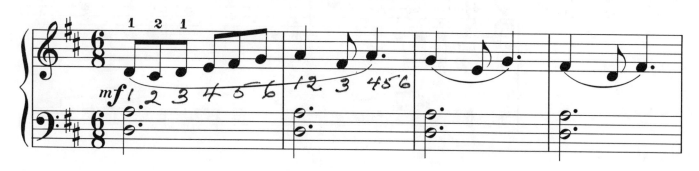

If Kangaroos Danced

With bounce

If the kan-ga- roo could dance, what do you think? How would he do?

If the kan-ga- roo could dance, what do you think? How do you think he would do?!

Grasshoppers

Cobbler, Cobbler

Warm-ups for daily practice. See page 64, Unit 8.

Rhythm In each of the following rhythms, set a strong rhythmic pulse:
  Point and count.
  Tap and count.

Writing Write intervals *down* from the starting note.
  Then write the name of the last note in each measure.
  (Your answers should spell a word.)

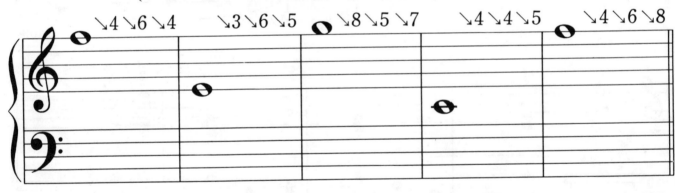

Accompanying and Transposing Accompany this melody with 5ths and 6ths.
  Then transpose to C major.

Humming

UNIT NINE

DISCOVERY: *Crossing Finger 3 over the Thumb*

To the Fair

Rock Climbing

Add the optional accompaniment (in small notes) only after
the crossings in the melody are smooth and easy.

USING WHAT YOU HAVE DISCOVERED

A Game

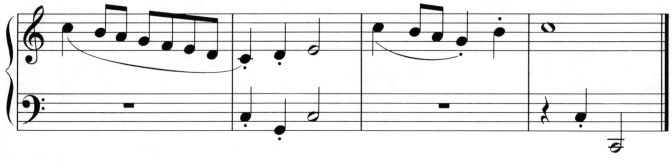

In the Pirate's Cave

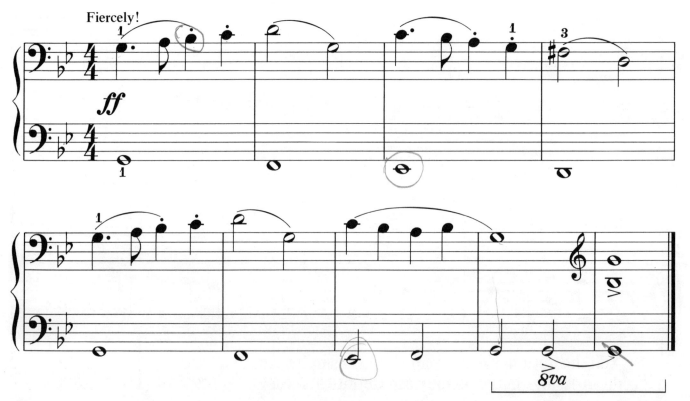

Row, Row, Row Your Boat

Traditional

Gondolier

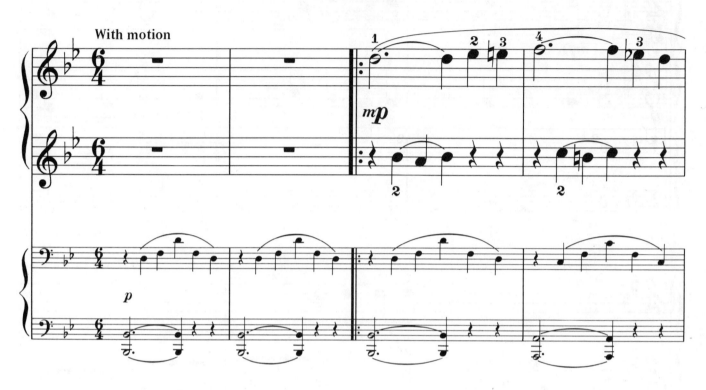

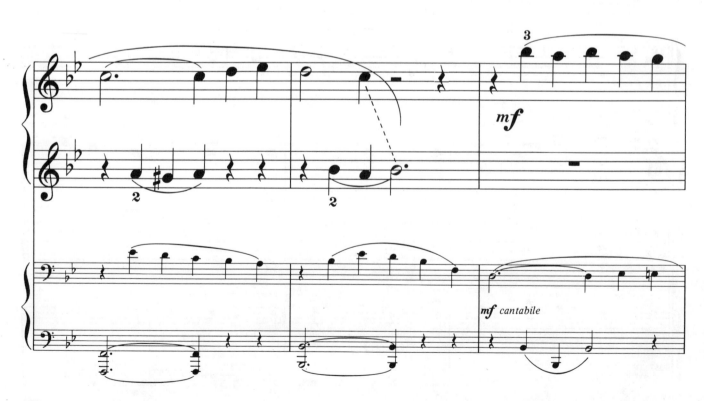

53

Warm-ups for daily practice.   See page 64, Unit 9.

Rhythm

In each of the following rhythms, set a strong rhythmic pulse:
Point and count hands separately.
Tap and count hands together.

Accompanying and Transposing

Accompany this melody with 5ths and 6ths.
Then transpose to the key of D major.

Rosa

Dutch

UNIT TEN

DISCOVERY: *Sliding the Thumb Under*

Up and Away

Drifting

Add the optional accompaniment (in small notes) only after
the crossings in the melody are smooth and easy.

USING WHAT YOU HAVE DISCOVERED

Mighty Proud

Gray Day

Yodelling

Holiday Bells

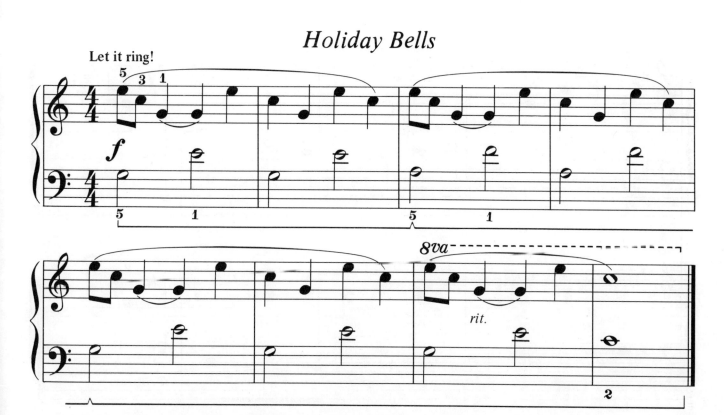

Round-Up Time

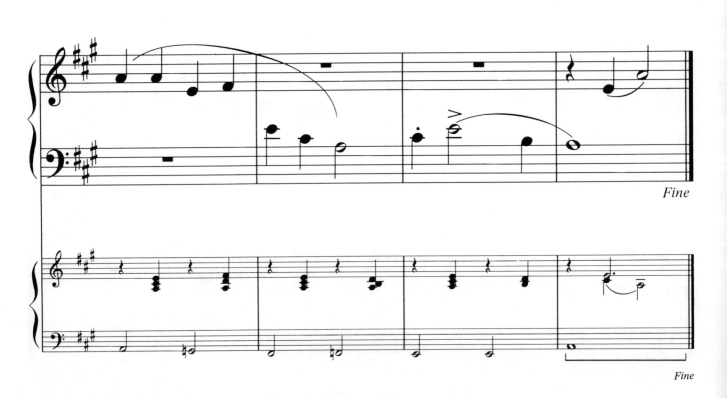

Fine

Fine

D.C. al Fine

59

Warm-ups for daily practice. See page 64, Unit 10.

Rhythm

In each of the following rhythms, set a strong rhythmic pulse:
Tap and count hands together.

Writing

Write intervals *up* from the starting note.
Then write the name of the last note in each measure.
(Your answers should spell a word.)

Write intervals *down* from the starting note.
Then write the name of the last note in each measure.
   (Your answers should spell a word.)

Accompanying and Transposing

Accompany this melody with 5ths and 6ths—
   notice that the first line is in G major,
   the second line in D major.

Then transpose the melody with your accompaniment:
   the first line to F major, the second line to C major.

London's Bells

English

Fine

D.C. al Fine

TECHNICAL WARM-UPS

To the Teacher:

Technical Goals for Part C

The goals are the same as for Parts A and B, with these additions:

    Learning to play 6ths (blocked and broken)

    Learning to move back and forth easily from 5ths to 6ths.

    Developing control in scale-like passages:

        crossing finger 2 over the thumb

        crossing finger 3 over the thumb

        sliding the thumb under

Teaching Suggestions

1. It is important to go over each pattern with the student the day it is assigned, setting standards for:

How the tone should sound

How the hand should look while playing

How the hand and body should feel to produce the sound

2. The emphasis on coordination between the hands, introduced in Part B, continues in Part C.

    The patterns written on a *single staff* are written in the treble clef if they are for RH, in the bass clef if for LH. If finger numbers appear both above and below the pattern, it should be learned RH alone, then LH alone one or two octaves lower. If the pattern is also to be practiced hands together, there is a special instruction.

UNIT 1 Play pattern RH alone, L.H alone, then hands together

Transpose to the keys of C major, F major, A major, and E major.

UNIT 2

UNIT 3

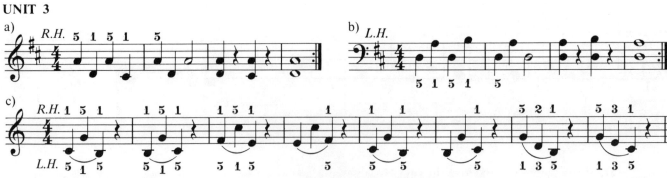

Transpose patterns a) and b) to the keys of G major and C major.

UNIT 4

a)

b)

Play pattern c) RH alone, LH alone, then hands together.

c)

Transpose patterns a) and b) to the key of G major.
Transpose pattern c) to the keys of D major and F major.

UNIT 5

a)

b)

UNIT 6

Play, beginning on every white key from C to C.

Transpose patterns a) and b) to the key of G major.
Transpose patterns c) and d) to the keys of G major, A major, and E major.

UNIT 7

a)
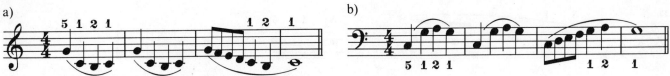
b)

Transpose both patterns to the keys of A major and E major.

UNIT 8

a)
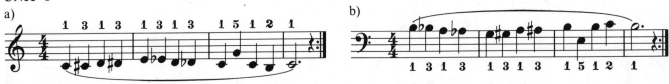
b)

UNIT 9

a)

b)

Play pattern c) RH alone, LH alone, then hands together.

c)

Transpose pattern c) to the keys of D major, F major, and E major.

UNIT 10

a)

b)

c)

d)

64